W9-BIA-543

Simple Sashiko

8 SASHIKO SEWING PROJECTS FOR THE MODERN HOME

SUSAN BRISCOE

David and Charles

www.stitchcraftcreate.co.uk

Contents

Introduction

Sashiko is the simple yet evocative stitching tradition of northern Japan. Pronounced 'sash(i)ko' (the 'i' is almost silent), it means 'little stab' or 'little pierce' – an accurate description of the stitching action. Originally invented for the thrifty creation of warm garments, made with recycled indigo fabric and conserving as much thread as possible, sashiko has developed into the richly patterned and often brightly coloured designs of today.

Simple Sashiko contains everything you need to know to get started in this creative, satisfying and often rather therapeutic style of embroidery. Each project includes simple instructions for marking and stitching the authentic designs, and for turning them into a range of beautiful items. This book will launch you into a life-long love of Japanese artistry as you capture the magic of sashiko in your work.

Getting Started

This section contains all the technical information you need to create beautiful sashiko. It will help you choose suitable tools, equipment and materials. The basic information on how to mark the patterns, stitching and finishing your work are all included – essential sashiko know-how at your fingertips.

TOOLS AND MATERIALS

Sashiko requires only basic sewing equipment and materials, and you will probably already have a basic sewing kit (see below) which can all be used.

» Sewing & marking kit

› Sashiko needles (various sizes)

› Sewing needles 'sharps'

› Small embroidery scissors

› Dressmaking scissors

› Pincushion or needle case

› Pins

› Thimble (optional)

› Tacking (basting) thread

› Sewing thread to match your fabrics

› Marking tools, including markers for dark and light fabrics, rulers and templates for marking curved designs.

› Rulers – ordinary and quilter's

» Cutting mat and quilter's ruler

These are excellent for precision marking. You might also prefer to cut out your fabrics with a rotary cutter.

» Japanese embroidery scissors

Nigiri basami are not essential, but do make sewing sashiko feel very authentic! They are also useful for snipping threads at the sewing machine.

» Sewing machine

This is useful for assembling projects, although old sashiko items were made completely by hand. Zigzag as well as straight stitching will be useful, as fabrics suitable for sashiko tend to fray and it is a good idea to zigzag the edges before you begin hand stitching, especially with larger projects that will be handled a lot.

NEEDLES

Sashiko needles are, compared with ordinary Western sewing needles, quite thick and rigid in relation to their length. They are also sharp. Very long needles will help keep your stitching lines straight and speed up your sewing, once you are used to them. If you normally hand quilt with 'Betweens' (special short quilting needles), you may find the smaller sashiko needles easier to manage at first, although the smallest are only suitable for fine sashiko thread. If sashiko needles are unavailable, try embroidery crewels or larger darning needles.

Match your sashiko needle to the thread and fabric weight. Finer threads and smaller needles will work with slightly heavier fabrics but it will be difficult to stitch a thick sashiko thread with a large needle through finer fabrics. If sashiko feels like hard work, change to a finer thread and needle or to a fabric with a lower thread count.

THREAD

Sashiko thread was specially spun, although ordinary fabric and needles were originally used. Modern sashiko thread has a looser twist than many embroidery threads and is made from long staple cotton. It is therefore very hardwearing and strong – you can't snap it! Various brands are sold worldwide, in large skeins and in several weights – fine, medium and thick – in a rainbow of colours and shaded effects as well as white, cream and indigo. The exact thickness and shade varies between manufacturers, so use the same brand throughout a sashiko project. One 100m skein of sashiko thread in white or cream, plus smaller amounts of coloured threads, will be enough for several projects. Thread quantities given in the projects are fairly generous.

If you cannot obtain real sashiko thread, cotton à broder makes a reasonable substitute. Cotton perlé does not really look or behave like sashiko thread, although it can add an interesting colour accent. Thread made for sashiko will give you the best results as a beginner and you can experiment to find other suitable threads later on, once you know what sashiko thread looks and feels like. To create additional colours, thread can be dyed at home, either with natural or synthetic dyes

FABRICS

Sashiko was originally stitched on cotton, linen, hemp and other plant fibres. Copies of old hand-woven fabrics are specially made for sashiko, in indigo and other shades (see Suppliers). Fabric and threads often echo natural dyes and 'antique' colours. Choose plain weaves and natural fibres with a lower thread count (the number of threads to the inch), slightly thicker than you might normally choose for quilting. Some quilting and craft fabrics, such as prairie cloth, 'Osnaburg' cloth and cotton flannel, are pleasant to stitch and look authentic. Indian cottons made for household textiles are an excellent source of thicker cottons and dressmaking fabrics can be used too. Old sashiko was often stitched on recycled fabrics, so that's another option, but always check that old fabrics are still strong enough to use.

FABRIC MARKERS

Marking your chosen sashiko pattern on the fabric will be easy with the right marker. Choose a marker you like and marking will be a pleasure.

HERA

The Japanese sewing marker, traditionally made of bone (and now plastic), scores and polishes a line on the cloth. It shows up best on very dark fabrics and the line washes out. Always put a cutting mat or cardboard under your fabric when marking or you will permanently score your table!

QUILTER'S WHITE PENCIL

This soft pencil is good for dark fabrics, with marks that wash out or rub off. Sharpen soft pencils with a craft knife, cutting away on either side and trimming to make a flat point – the pencil will last much longer.

AIR-ERASABLE MARKING PEN (WHITE)

This is a felt-tip pen that marks white and fades away when exposed to air. The marks only last for 48 hours and can fade sooner, so use it for small projects. Remember to wash out the chemical residue when the work is complete.

WHITE MARKING PEN

This is a roller ball that makes a fine, clear white line which takes a few seconds to 'develop' after drawing. Marks can be removed with water or heat (check individual brand information).

QUILTER'S SILVER PENCIL

This is best for light fabrics, as the marks can be difficult to see on dark or medium colours. Marks wash out or rub off. Blue marking pens are another option but must be washed out or the chemicals may damage fabric.

TAILOR'S CHALK

This is an inexpensive marker available in various colours. Marks brush off easily but can be redrawn. It washes out.

BASIC TECHNIQUES

Here are the basic sashiko techniques, from tacking (basting) fabric layers together, to how to complete the stitching and finish your work.

MARKING THE PATTERNS

You can mark the pattern directly on to the top fabric or draw the design on paper and transfer it. Pictorial designs must be traced or photocopied before transferring the pattern. Use the parallel lines on a quilter's ruler to mark the base grid for the pattern and mark directly on the fabric **(A)**. Allow for the width of the line if marking with tailor's chalk – the line can be up to ⅛in thick, so line up with the bottom of each line or your grid might be 1⅛in not 1in!

Alternatively, use the grid on a cutting mat to mark the base grid and mark directly on the fabric **(B)**. Some mats have both imperial and metric grids and you can use an ordinary ruler. The fabric will need to be smaller than the mat, so you can see the mat grid all round the edge, and the ruler should be long enough to reach the opposite sides of the mat. If you don't have a cutting mat, a large sheet of graph paper can be used instead.

TACKING (BASTING) FABRIC LAYERS

Once you have marked your fabric with your sashiko pattern you can prepare the fabric for sewing. If you are using butter muslin, or other loose cotton scrim backing, lay the sashiko fabric right side up on top of it and tack (baste) the layers together vertically and horizontally at about 3in (7.6cm) intervals.

Rather than binding the edges, most projects in this book are 'bagged out', by placing the backing and sashiko right sides together, stitching round the edge and turning the item right side out through a gap left in the stitching. If wadding is added, this means layering the wadding first, then the backing and finally the top, which is then tied, not quilted.

USING SASHIKO THREAD

First open out the skein and remove the paper band. Look for the extra loop of thread tied around the skein and cut through all the threads at this point **(C)**. The threads will seem very long but don't cut them. Sashiko skeins are made to just the right length for using the thread. Hold the other end of the skein and loosely plait the threads to keep them tidy **(D)**. Draw out individual threads from the top of the plait.

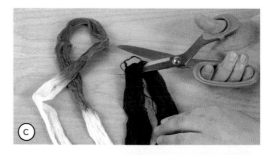

STARTING AND FINISHING SASHIKO STITCHING

When you have marked your sashiko pattern on your fabric and tacked (basted) the fabric layers together you are ready to begin stitching the sashiko. First, thread your needle with a single length of thread. Pull the two ends together and smooth down the thread to remove any excess twist. Holding the thread taut between your hands and twanging it with your thumbs is said to get the excess twist out too! Remember, stitching with doubled thread gives traditional sashiko the 'big stitch' look that is so attractive. It also means that there is no loose end to become frayed and worn during stitching.

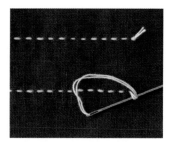

Starting and finishing with a knot (shown from the back of the stitching).

STARTING AND FINISHING WITH A KNOT

Begin by holding the two ends together and tying an ordinary single knot (sometimes called a quilter's knot). Begin stitching with the single knot on the back of your work. The knots don't show on the front. When you get to the end, take the needle to the back and wrap the thread around it once. Hold this point between your thumb and forefinger, so the knot can't travel further up the thread, and pull the needle through. If you have left yourself with too little thread to do this, remember you only need about 2.5cm (1in) of thread to tie the knot with the eye end of the needle. This method also uses a hatamusubi knot to join in new threads.

MAKING A HATAMUSUBI (LOOM KNOT)

In Japan in the past, thread was precious so a hatamusubi (joining knot) was used to get the most out of even the last half inch. The harder this knot is pulled, the tighter it becomes. To make tying the knot easier, moisten the ends of the doubled thread so they stick together. The method is the same for right and left-handed people – both hands do equal amounts of work! The secret is in the way the short ends of thread are held whilst the knot is tied. Practise using different coloured threads.

1. Leave a 1in (2.5cm) tail of old thread loose on the back of work (shown in white). Thread the needle but do not knot the new thread. Lay the end(s) of the new thread (shown in red) against the back of the work.

2. Hold the end of the new thread between the first two fingers of your left hand (at point A). Use your left thumb to bend the tail of the old thread over the new. Put your thumb on the crossed threads to hold them. Keep holding these two points until instructed otherwise.

3. Now the long part of the new thread does most of the work. Loop it to the left, as shown by the arrow. Lift your thumb quickly, pass the thread under it and hold the crossed threads firmly again.

4. Take the long part of the new thread under its own tail and over the old thread. At this point you will see that the new thread has made a loop.

5. Continue to hold the thread at point A. Use your right index finger to bend the old thread through the loop and hold the end between your left thumb and left ring finger at point B. Holding the two short ends so they can't flip out of the knot, use the long new thread to gently pull the knot closed with your right hand.

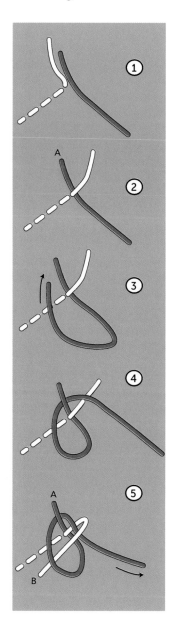

SEWING SASHIKO

In Japanese sewing, the needle is held still and the fabric placed on it in a pleating action, several stitches at a time, rather than making individual stitches with the needle being moved through fixed fabric. A quilting frame or hoop is not used for sashiko and it is not stitched from the centre outwards, like Western quilting, but from one side to the other.

Begin stitching at one side of the pattern and work your way across. Traditionally, a kakehari (or 'third hand') is used to hold large pieces of fabric under tension and you might like to try this.

Push the needle through when it is full and smooth the stitches out between your thumb and forefinger, but don't fluff up the thread by scraping it with your nails. This is how to make stitches where the double thread will lie parallel, making patterns appear quite bold and creating a textured effect because the stitches are slightly raised.

Taking one stitch at a time will twist the threads and spoil your sashiko, so try to take several stitches whenever possible, even on pictorial designs. You can use a coin thimble to help push the needle through thicker projects or just hold the needle as you would normally – it isn't necessary to hold the needle in the traditional Japanese way to sew good sashiko.

The needle going into the fabric and taking several stitches.

Needle coming out of the fabric.

Pulling the thread through and gathering up.

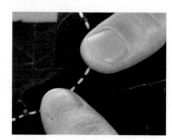

Easing the gathers out.

SASHIKO STITCHING TIPS

Watch out for the following points when stitching designs.

1. When turning corners, make the last stitch right into the corner so the pattern is sharply defined.

2. Where pattern lines meet, space the stitches so they don't touch each other.

3. Where indicated in some patterns, you will need to strand loosely across the back of your work. For a quilt where the back will be seen, run the thread between the backing and wadding.

4. Where pattern lines cross, make a slightly longer gap between stitches, so stitches don't cross on the right side, making an ugly lump (and a weak point). Avoid joining in new threads at these points.

5. When you make a sharp change of direction, leave a little loop on the back for ease.

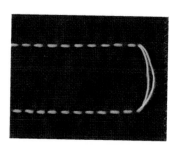

Stranding loosely across the back of the work prevents your sashiko stitches pulling too tightly and distorting the fabric.

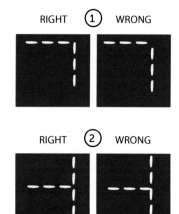

RIGHT ① WRONG

RIGHT ② WRONG

RIGHT ③ WRONG

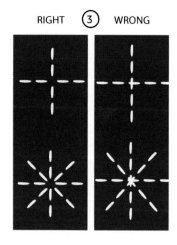

RIGHT ④ WRONG

RIGHT ⑤ WRONG

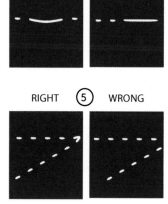

FRAMING

Some of the designs have been made up as wall hangings but they could also be framed. In fact, framing your sashiko is probably the easiest way to finish a panel and make your work look really professional.

1. Remove any glass from the frame and the backing panel. Two sides may need trimming down, as the thick sashiko fabric will need to wrap over the edges.

2. Lay the panel right side down on a clean, flat surface and place the backing panel on it centrally. Using a very long length of thread, lace the panel across the back of the frame, horizontally and vertically. You can join extra thread using a hatamusubi knot. Don't pull the panel too tight.

3. Check the sashiko is square before replacing the board in the frame. If there is glass, clean it so dust is not trapped between the glass and sashiko. Lay the frame flat, put the glass in, then the panel and fold the backing pins back over the panel.

MAKING A HANGING SLEEVE

Using a remaining strip of fabric, turn under the ends and hem. With wrong sides together, fold in half lengthwise and machine sew. Don't turn the sleeve inside out – the seam will be hidden when sewn to the hanging. Press the sleeve flat, with the seam open and centred along one side. Pin the sleeve to the back of the hanging, ½in (1.3cm) from the top edge and centred. The sleeve will be shorter than the hanging. Hand sew the sleeve to the hanging, keeping stitches invisible from the front.

Asanoha tote bag

The Asanoha (hemp leaf) pattern lends itself beautifully to this handy tote bag, for Japanese living on the go!

Sashiko pattern used asanoha (hemp leaf) variation

Finished size 15 x 12in (38.1 x 30.5cm)

If your piece of sashiko fabric is slightly smaller, resize the outer patchwork panel. Make a sketch to note down the new fabric sizes. Use the finished outer panel as a pattern to cut the lining. You can resize the bag very easily

You will need

- » Sashiko fabric 10½ x 7½in (26.7 x 19cm)

- » Thick cotton fabric:
  - › one strip 18½ x 13in (47 x 33cm), one strip 3¼ x 13in (8.3 x 33cm),
  - › two strips 10½ x 3¼in (26.7 x 8.3cm), two strips 13 x 4in (33 x 10.2cm) for handles

- » Plain cotton 31 x 13in (78.7 x 33cm) for lining

- » Approximately 4 strands of medium sashiko thread in cream or white

- » Sewing thread

- » Basic sewing and marking kit

MARKING AND STITCHING

1. Zigzag or overlock all the patchwork pieces before you begin. Mark a rectangle on the sashiko fabric ½in (1.3cm) inside all the edges. Following **(A)**, quarter the rectangle equally into four smaller rectangles, then equally again into eight rectangles.

2. Mark zigzag lines, as shown by the heavy black lines in diagrams 3 and 4. Stitch the sashiko, following the red arrows in 3, 4, and 5. Refer to the stitching tips within the Getting Started section. Press the completed panel.

ASSEMBLING THE PATCHWORK

3. Machine sew the patchwork, as shown in **(B)**, using ¼in (6mm) seams throughout.

4. Sew the two 10½ x 3¼in (26.7 x 8.3cm) strips to either side of the sashiko panel and press towards the strips. Sew the largest piece to one end of the patchwork and the 13 x 3¼in (33 x 8.3cm) strip to the other end and press.

MAKING THE HANDLES

5. Following **(C)**, fold and press the first handle strip in half lengthways. Fold the long edges inwards to the pressed line, press again, then fold the long edges into the middle and press. Machine sew along each long edge, about 1⁄16in (2mm) from the edge. Zigzag the ends. Repeat with the other strip. Turn under ¼in (6mm) hem twice along one long side of each pocket piece and machine sew.

ASSEMBLING THE BAG

6. Temporarily fold the bag panel in half, right sides outside, so the top of the bag meets. Arrange the handles on the right side of the bag panel as shown in **(D)**, allowing the handle ends to overlap the edge of the bag panel by ½in (1.3cm).

6. Repeat for the back of the bag. The gap between the handle ends is 4in (10.2cm) on each side. Make sure the handles are the same length and not twisted. Tack (baste) in place.

7. With the bag panel folded right sides together and using a ½in (1.3cm) seam, machine sew down the sides of the bag, shown by the dashed lines in **(E)**.

8. Clip the corners within the seam allowance but don't cut right up to the stitches – leave about 1⁄8in (3mm). Press the side seams open.

9. Make the lining by folding the lining fabric in half, right sides together and, with a ½in (1.3cm) seam, machine sew down both sides, as shown in **(F)**.

10. Leave a 4in (10.2cm) gap unsewn in the second side. The bag will be turned right side out through the unsewn gap. Press the seams open.

11. Turn the outer bag section right side out. Keeping the bag lining turned inside out, place the bag outer inside the lining, aligning the top edge and the side seams. Machine sew around the top of the bag, sewing the lining to the bag outer all round with a ½in (1.3cm) seam. Turn the bag right side out, through the unsewn gap in the lining side seam. Press the seam at the top of the bag. Machine or hand sew around the top of the bag, about 1⁄8in (3mm) from the edge. Turn the bag inside out and slipstitch the gap in the lining closed.

12. Push the bottom corners of the lining into the bottom corners of the bag. Tack (baste) the lining to the outside of the bag for about 4in (10.2cm) at the bottom corners. Fold the corners to make a point, as shown in **(G)**.

13. Mark a line at right angles to the seam, 2in (5cm) from the point, then pin and machine sew across, sewing the bottom corner of the bag and lining together and creating a triangular flap of fabric. Fold this flap up against the side seam and use sashiko stitches to stitch the flap to the bag, ¼in (6mm) from the edge, sewing right through the lining. To finish, slipstitch the edges of the flap to the bag to neaten.

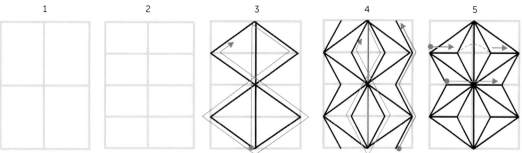

A) 1-5 Asanoha variation: The sequence for marking and stitching the pattern to fit a rectangle

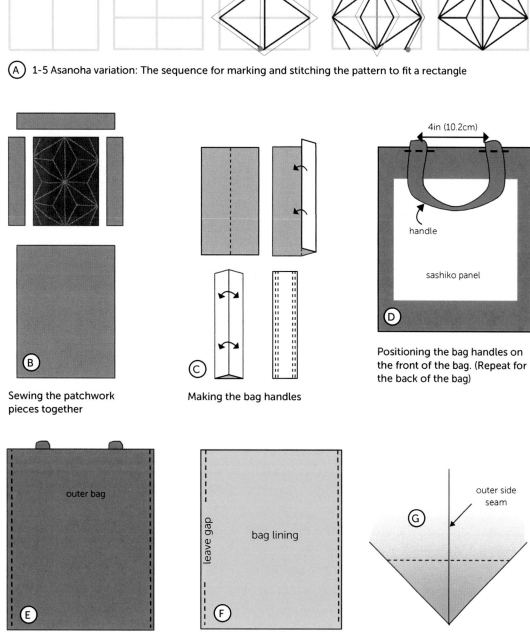

B) Sewing the patchwork pieces together

C) Making the bag handles

D) Positioning the bag handles on the front of the bag. (Repeat for the back of the bag)

handle

sashiko panel

4in (10.2cm)

E) Sewing up the sides of the bag

outer bag

F) Making the bag lining

bag lining

leave gap

G) Creating the bag corners

outer side seam

Greetings cards

New Year celebrations in Japan rival Christmas in Europe and the USA but whatever the festive occasion a handmade greetings card is always extra special. These pretty cards use 4in (10.2cm) square samples of sashiko for a bold graphic effect. You can resize the sashiko pattern to fit other aperture sizes.

Sashiko patterns used Single asanoha and ganzezashi

Finished size of card 5in (12.7cm) square with 3in (7.6cm) aperture

You will need

» Card blank, photograph frame or other item with aperture to fit your embroidery

» Piece of sashiko fabric at least ½in (1.3cm) larger than aperture size all round

» Lightweight iron-on interfacing, same size as sashiko fabric

» Fine or medium sashiko thread in white or cream, 3 strands per card

» Masking tape or double-sided adhesive tape

» Basic sewing and marking kit

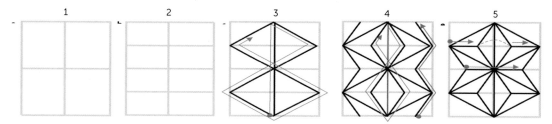

(A) 1-5 Asanoha variation: The sequence for marking and stitching the pattern to fit a rectangle.

PREPARING YOUR FABRIC

Zigzag or overlock all the sashiko pieces before you begin. Mark a square on the sashiko fabric the same size as the card aperture inside all the edges.

ASANOHA (HEMP LEAF)

Following **A**, quarter the rectangle equally into four smaller rectangles, then equally again into eight rectangles. Mark zigzag lines, as shown by the heavy black lines in diagrams 3 and 4. Stitch the sashiko, following the red arrows in 3, 4, and 5. Refer to the stitching tips within Getting Started. Press the completed panel.

GANZEZASHI (SEA URCHIN STITCH)

Extra lines can be added to give multiple diamond zigzags. The sample stitched on cream has just two zig-zag lines forming the diamonds, but the sashiko on blue in the card has four.

Mark a grid – the stitched sample is 1½in (3.2cm). Mark diagonal lines. Mark the zigzag lines using the dashed line in diagram **B** as a guide. Following the red arrows, stitch vertical lines, shown in red on the stitched sample. Stitch horizontal lines (shown in light brown) and then the diagonal lines (yellow and light green). Work the diamond zigzags in a continuous line around the pattern (dark brown and dark green).

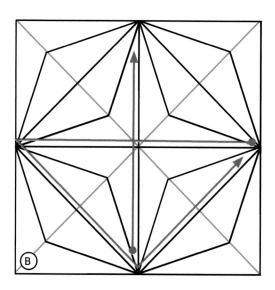

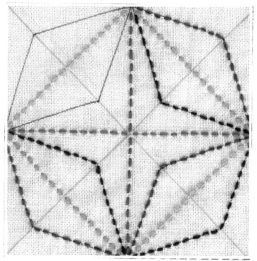

MARKING AND STITCHING THE SASHIKO

1. Use the inside of the card aperture or photograph frame as a stencil to mark the working area on your fabric. Select a design and mark the fabric, then stitch your sashiko design (see Getting Started).

2. Lightly press your finished sashiko from the back. Following the manufacturer's instructions, iron the interfacing on to the back of the sashiko. Trim raw edges back to the interfacing if necessary.

3. To mount the sashiko into a card, open out the card blank, arrange the sashiko behind the card aperture and use masking tape to hold it in place. If you are using a double-fold card blank as shown in **C**, the extra fold will hide the back of the sashiko. If your card has a single fold, shown in **D**, use a piece of paper and double-sided tape to cover the back of the sashiko neatly.

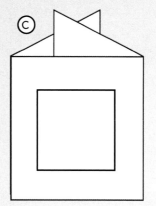

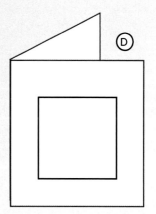

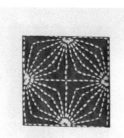

Blue sampler cushion

Stitch this cushion and add some Japanese style to your home or office space. Some sashiko patterns fit together very well for more elaborate arrangements as this striking cushion shows. Choose patterns that share the same base grid and they will fit together with ease. The cushion is patterned with five different hexagon and diamond designs on a ¾ x ⅜in (1.9 x 1cm) grid. The sashiko has been stitched through two layers, with muslin stabilizing the raw silk, or you can use a single layer of cotton fabric.

You will need

» Blue raw fabric 19in (48.3cm) square

» Piece of butter muslin, slightly larger than the silk

» Medium variegated or plain colour sashiko thread, approximately 40m

» Sewing thread to tone with fabrics

» Basic sewing and marking kit

» Two pieces of toning silk dupion 19 x 12in (48.3 x 30.5cm), for the cushion back

» Cushion pad 18in (45.7cm) square

» Sewing machine

Sashiko patterns used

Blue cushion (top to bottom) – hishi moyō , kasane kikkō, ju-ji kikkō, arare kikkō and yosegi

Finished cushion size 18in (45.7cm) square

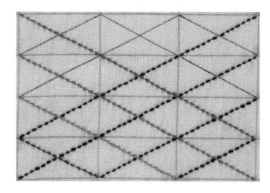

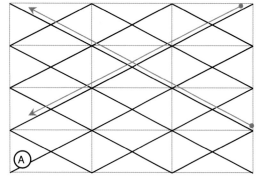

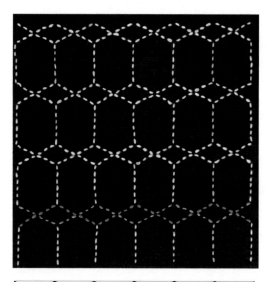

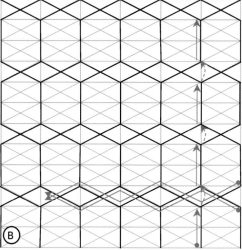

HISHI MOYŌ (DIAMOND PATTERN)

This forms the basis for all the patterns in this section, whether the stitches form continuous lines, broken lines or a varied shape.

To mark each diagonal grid **(A)**, start with a rectangular grid on a 2:1 ratio and fill it with diagonal lines. Each pattern gives an appropriate grid size.

Mark a grid – stitched sample is a 1 x 2in (2.5 x 5.1cm) diagonal grid. Following the red arrows, stitch diagonal lines in one direction (shown in red, light brown, yellow and green on the sample) and then the other direction (dark brown).

> The sample patterns have been stitched on various grid sizes but for the cushion a ¾ x ⅜ inch (1.9 x 1cm) grid is used for all the patterns. Each design could be used individually for an all-over pattern instead of the sampler arrangement.

KASANE KIKKŌ (LAYERED TORTOISESHELL)

This pattern is also known as kikkō hishi tsunagi (linked diamond tortoiseshell). Do you see the pattern as overlapping hexagons or long hexagons with diamonds? The latter gives a better clue as to how it is stitched – as horizontal lines of diamonds, linked with vertical lines to make the pattern.

Mark a grid – the stitched sample is a ½ x 1in (1.3 x 2.5cm) diagonal grid. Following the red arrows on diagram **B**, stitch the first horizontal zigzag lines (red), then the second horizontal zigzag lines (light brown). Stitch remaining vertical sections (yellow), keeping thread continuous.

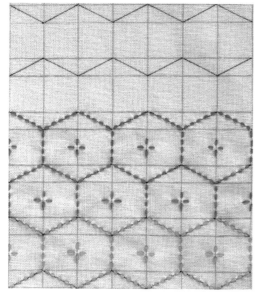

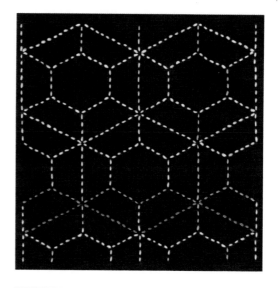

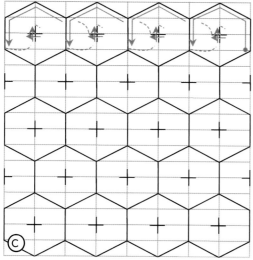

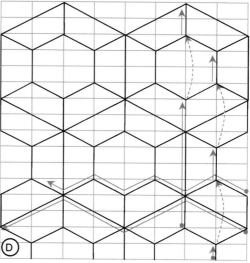

JŪJI KIKKŌ (CROSS TORTOISESHELL)

The sashiko pattern is worked in rows. Draw extra horizontal lines (optional) to keep the centre crosses straight.

Mark a grid – the stitched sample is ⅜ x ¾in (8mm x 1.9cm). Mark diagonal lines to form the tops of the hexagons. Following the red arrows **(C)**, stitch the pattern in rows, stitching around three sides of the hexagon (shown in red on the stitched sample), keeping the thread continuous and stranding across the back to stitch the centre crosses, indicated in the diagram by red dashed lines.

ARARE KIKKŌ (HAILSTONE OR SEGMENTED TORTOISESHELL)

This kikkō pattern has two sizes of hexagon superimposed on top of one another.

Mark a grid – the stitched sample is ⅜ x ¾in (8mm x 1.9cm) diagonal grid. Following the red arrows **(D)**, stitch horizontal zigzag lines (red). Stitch smaller zigzag lines (light brown) then short vertical lines (yellow), keeping thread continuous and stranding across the back. Stitch longer vertical lines (green) keeping thread continuous, as before.

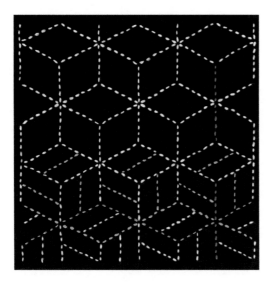

MARKING AND STITCHING THE SASHIKO

1. Tack (baste) the piece of muslin to the back of the raw silk and zigzag the edges to prevent fraying (see tacking in Getting Started). Mark and stitch the sashiko by first marking a ¾ x ⅜in (1.9cm x 8mm) diagonal grid in an 18in (45.7cm) square area on the raw silk, leaving a ½in (1.3cm) seam allowance all round (see marking in Getting Started). The pattern layout for the blue cushion is shown in **(F)** below. Stitch sashiko through both layers and, when finished, lightly press the sashiko from the wrong side.

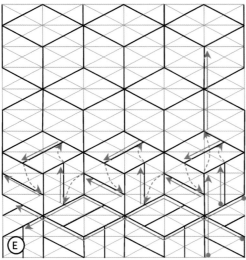

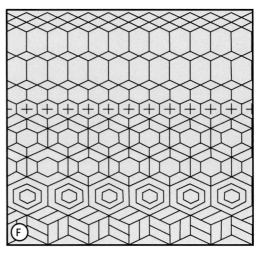

Blue cushion patterns.
All these patterns were drawn on a ¾ x ⅜in (1.9 x 1cm) diagonal grid. From top to bottom: hishi moyō (diamond pattern), kasane kikkō (layered tortoiseshell diamonds), jūji kikkō ('10' cross tortoiseshell), arare kikkō (hailstone or segmented tortoiseshell) and yosegi (mosaic or parquetry blocks).

YOSEGI (MOSAIC OR PARQUETRY BLOCKS)

These patterns have recently been used for patchwork quilts. The top of the sashiko sample has been left unfinished to make hakozashi (box stitch)

Mark a grid – the stitched sample is a ½ x 1in (1.3 x 2.5cm) diagonal grid. Following the red arrows **(E)**, stitch vertical lines (red), then horizontal zigzag lines (light brown and yellow). Finish by stitching the remaining angled lines (green), keeping thread continuous and stranding across the back.

G

first piece of
backing fabric
(right side down)

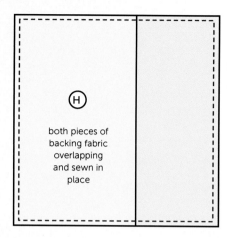

H

both pieces of
backing fabric
overlapping
and sewn in
place

2. Making up the cushion: Assemble the cushion, using ½in (1.3cm) seams throughout. Turn a ¼in (6mm) hem along one of the long sides on each piece of backing fabric. Zigzag the remaining raw edges. Place the sashiko and one backing piece right sides together and pin, as shown in **(G)**. Pin the second backing piece right sides together and overlapping the first piece **(H)**.

3. Machine sew around the edges, with ½in (6mm) seam allowance, leaving a gap for turning. Clip the corners, turn right side out and insert the cushion pad through the gap to finish.

Momoyama table mat & maple leaf coaster

This elegant table mat and coaster combine a diamond-based sashiko pattern and a momiji (maple leaf) motif. The maple has a special place in Japanese culture, where going to view maple trees in their autumn foliage is a popular tradition. Having the backing fabric showing slightly at the sides of the table mat, contrasting with the main colour, is a feature copied from lined kimono hems.

TABLE MAT

Sashiko patterns used
Hishi seigaiha and momiji

Finished size of mat
12 x 14in (30.5 x 35.5cm)

You will need

» Sashiko fabric 13 x 15in
(33 x 38cm)

» Backing fabric 13 x 15½in
(33 x 39.4cm)

» Butter muslin, slightly
larger than sashiko
fabric (optional)

» Sashiko thread in
medium cream, 20m skein

» Medium coloured or
variegated sashiko thread,
20m skein

» Sewing thread to tone with
fabric

» Basic sewing and marking kit

» Sewing machine

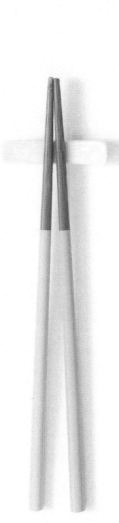

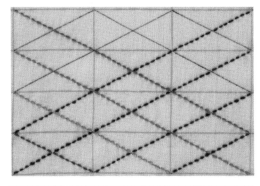

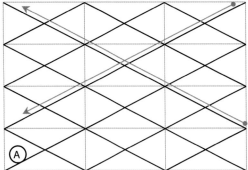

HISHI MOYŌ (DIAMOND PATTERN)

This forms the basis for the hishi seigaiha patterns in this section, whether the stitches form continuous lines, broken lines or a varied shape.

To mark each diagonal grid, start with a rectangular grid on a 2:1 ratio and fill it with diagonal lines. Each pattern gives an appropriate grid size.

Mark a grid – the sample is a 1 x 2in (2.5 x 5.1cm) diagonal grid. Following the red arrows, stitch diagonal lines in one direction (shown in red, light brown, yellow and green on the sample) and then the other direction (dark brown).

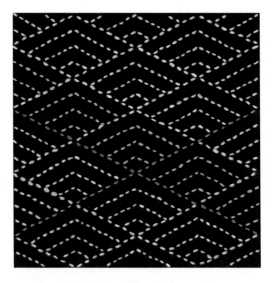

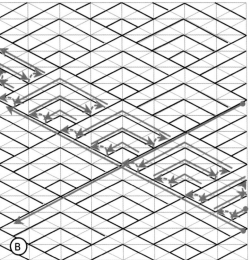

HISHI SEIGAIHA (DIAMOND BLUE WAVES)

Mark a grid – the sample is a ⅜ x ¾in (1 x 1.9cm) diagonal grid. Following the red arrows shown on diagram **B** and the instructions for hishi moyō, stitch diagonal lines to form a grid with diamonds 3in (7.6cm) wide (red and light brown). Fill in each diamond, back and forth (yellow), keeping thread continuous and stranding across the back.

MARKING AND STITCHING THE SASHIKO

1. Zigzag the edges of the sashiko fabrics to prevent fraying. On the fabric, mark a 1 x ½in (2.5 x 1.3cm) diagonal grid in an area 14 x 12in (35.6 x 30.5cm), leaving a ½in (1.3cm) seam allowance all round (see Marking in Getting Started). The large diamonds are 4 x 2in (10.2 x 5.1cm) – see **C** for basic layout.

2. If you are using a muslin layer, tack (baste) a piece of muslin to the back of the sashiko fabric and stitch the sashiko through both layers (see Tacking in Getting Started). Stitch the diamond pattern in cream thread. Mark and stitch the maple leaf detail **(D)**, which is shown here actual size, then stitch the background with diagonal lines, the same distance apart as the hishi seigaiha infill. Lightly press finished the sashiko from the wrong side.

MAKING UP A TABLE MAT

3. Place the front panel and the contrasting backing piece right sides together, and pin the ends only, lining up the cut edges **(E)**.

Note: the back panel will be longer than the front, so approximately ⅛in (3mm) will show at either end of the finished mat, echoing the thread colour. Sew the panel and backing together at the ends only, using ½in (1.3cm) seams. Press the seams towards the front panel as indicated in **E**.

4. Pin the top and bottom edges and machine sew together, leaving a 4in (10.2cm) gap in the centre of the lower edge. Trim off the corners within the seam allowance but do not cut right up to the stitches – about halfway is fine. Bag out the panel, i.e., turn it the right way out through the unsewn gap. Ease the corners out so they are nice and sharp. Lay the mat flat and smooth it out. The backing fabric will show as a narrow strip at the ends – hold it in place with small, neat hand stitches through backing and seam allowances only. Turn under the raw edges at the bottom of the mat, pin or tack (baste) and then slipstitch the gap closed.

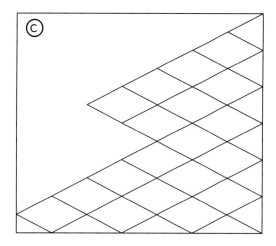

D MOMIJI (MAPLE)

press side seams towards
sashiko panel

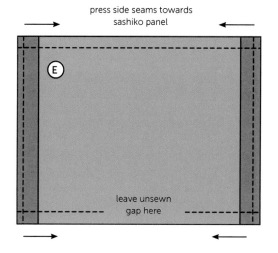

leave unsewn
gap here

COASTER

Sashiko patterns used
Maple leaf motif

Finished size of coaster
3½in (8.9cm) square

You will need

» Sashiko fabric 4in (10.2cm) square

» Square of butter muslin, slightly larger than sashiko square (optional)

» Patchwork cotton 4in (10.2cm) square, for backing

» 3 strands of fine or medium sashiko thread or variegated perlé thread

» Sewing thread to tone with fabric

» Basic sewing and marking kit

» Sewing machine

MARKING AND STITCHING THE SASHIKO

1. If you wish to use a muslin layer, tack (baste) a piece of muslin to the back of the sashiko fabric and stitch the sashiko pattern through both layers (see Getting Started). Mark and stitch the maple leaf motif **(A)** in sashiko or vareigated thread. Press lightly when all stitching is complete.

MAKING UP THE COASTER

2. Place a square of backing fabric right sides together with the sashiko square, pin and machine sew around the square with a ¼in (6mm) seam allowance, leaving 2½in (6.4cm) unsewn on one side. Snip the points off the corners, but do not cut right up to the stitches – leave about ⅛in (3mm). Turn the coaster right side out and push the corners out. Turn in the raw edges of the gap and slipstitch together invisibly. Press lightly.

3. Use scraps of variegated or plain thread to make simple corner 'tassels' as follows. Stitch into one of the seams at the corner of the coaster, through all the layers, following the arrows in diagram **B**, and leaving strands of approximately 1½in (3.2cm) long. Repeat once more to make a thin tassel. Tie all the strands together in a single knot, loosely at the corner, and then trim the thread ends to about 1in (2.5cm).

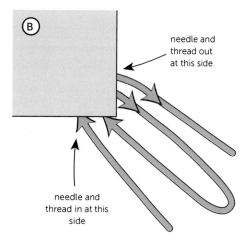

needle and thread out at this side

needle and thread in at this side

Ⓐ MOMIJI (MAPLE)

Tansu pocket hanging

Create this striking pocket hanging, stitched with beautiful sashiko, and hang it on a plain wall in your home office, your craft space or wherever takes your fancy. The pockets are a handy and unusual way to store all your crafty bits and pieces, a good home for pencils, crochet hooks, notebooks, knitting needles.

Sashiko patterns used: shippō (seven treasures) variations, shippō tsunagi (linked seven treasures), nowaki (grasses), seigaiha (ocean waves) and variation

Finished size: 14½ x 11½in (36.8 x 29.2cm)

You will need

» Sashiko fabric:
  › one piece 8½ x 10½in (21.6 x 26.7cm) for back of large pocket
  › one piece 15½ x 10½in (39.4 x 26.7cm) for front of large pocket
  › two pieces 5½ x 5¼in (14 x 13.3cm) for back of small pockets
  › two pieces 8½ x 5¼in (21.6 x 13.3cm) for front of small pockets
  › Cotton tsumugi or a dark plain cotton:
  › one piece 5½ x 1in (14 x 2.5cm) for between small pockets
  › one piece 10½ x 1in (26.7 x 2.5cm) for between small and large pockets

  › two pieces 14 x 1½in (35.6 x 3.8cm) for vertical borders
  › two pieces 12½ x 1½in (31.8 x 3.8cm) for horizontal borders
  › one piece 16 x 12½in (40.6 x 31.8cm) for backing

» Plain cotton strip 12 x 3in (30.5 x 7.6cm), for a hanging sleeve (see Getting Started)

» Medium sashiko thread, shaded blue to white, approximately 30m

» Sewing thread

» Basic sewing and marking kit

MARKING THE SASHIKO

1. Zigzag or overlock the edges of the sashiko panels. Take the 8½ x 5¼in (21.6 x 13.3cm) pieces for the two top pockets and fold each one in half and press to form the pocket. Draw a 4in (10.2cm) square in the centre of each pocket, with the top of the square on the pressed fold **(A)**.

2. Draw lines at 2in (5cm) intervals, quartering each square. Draw diagonal lines on each square. Now mark the two shippō variations, following **B** (right-hand pocket) and **C** (left-hand pocket).

3. Mark the pattern in **B** using a 4in (10.2cm) diameter circle to mark the interlocking semicircles and a 3in (7.6cm) circle for the inner circle. Mark the pattern in **C**, beginning with a 4in (10.2cm) circle centred on the square. Mark a 1in (2.5cm) circle in the centre, as a guideline for the curved points. Use a 5½in (14cm) diameter circle template to mark the curved points, linking the outer circle to the inner circle, as shown.

TO MARK THE MAIN SASHIKO PANEL

4. Fold the 15½ x 10½in (39.4 x 26.7cm) fabric piece in half and press to form the pocket. Mark the patterns as shown in **D**.

5. Draw a 1½in (3.2cm) grid in the centre of the pocket, with the top line of the grid on the pressed fold. Starting from the bottom of the grid and using a 2½in (6.4cm) diameter circle template, mark shippō tsunagi (a) over two rows by drawing overlapping circles.

6. Mark nowaki (b) by drawing semicircles, offset over two rows, adding the 'grasses' inside each semicircle, pivoting the circle template at the corner of each semicircle. Continue marking the offset semicircles to the top of the grid.

7. Complete the seigaiha variation pattern (c) by marking a second semicircle in each, using a 2in (5cm) diameter circle template, and adding a shallow arc at the bottom of that pattern using the same template.

8. Complete seigaiha (d) across the top row with a 2in (5cm) circle and 1½in (3.8cm) circle.

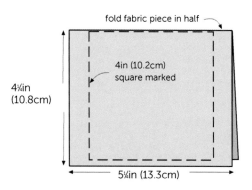

fold fabric piece in half

4in (10.2cm) square marked

4¼in (10.8cm)

5¼in (13.3cm)

(A) For the two top pockets, fold the fabric in half and mark a 4in (10.2cm) square.

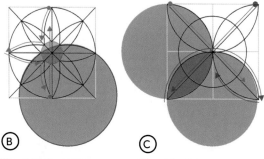

(B) The shippō variation pattern for the top right-hand pocket.

(C) The shippō (seven treasures) variation pattern for the top left-hand pocket.

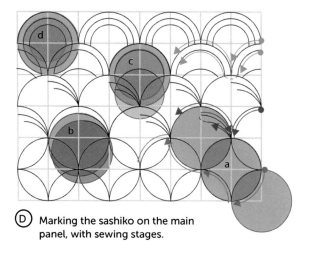

(D) Marking the sashiko on the main panel, with sewing stages.

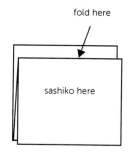

fold here

sashiko here

(E) **Arranging the folded sashiko panels.**

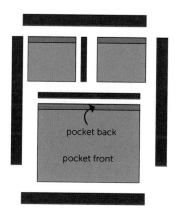

pocket back

pocket front

(F) **Sewing the patchwork pieces together.**

STITCHING THE SASHIKO

9. Open out the folded pocket panels and stitch through only one layer. Stitch the pattern in diagram **B** (right-hand pocket) by stitching the vertical, horizontal and diagonal lines first, crossing the centre. Stitch around the large circle, then the curved points, as indicated by the red arrows.

10. Stitch the pattern in **C** (left-hand pocket) by stitching the first diagonal line, as shown by the red arrow. Stitch the second diagonal line, as shown by blue arrow, then semicircles, working around the motif. Stitch the circle and then press the sashiko.

11. Begin stitching the larger pocket panel with the shippō section, at the bottom of the panel, following the red arrows in **D**, stitching in diagonal wavy lines. Next stitch the nowaki section, following the blue arrows, stitch across each semicircle and along the grasses, stranding across the back between the grasses as shown by the dashed blue line. Stitch seigaiha and its variation following the green arrows, stitching the outer semicircle first, then filling in the smaller semicircles, and stranding across the back as shown by the dashed green line. Press when finished.

MAKING THE PATCHWORK

12. Arrange the folded sashiko panels on the front of the remaining pieces, as in **E**, lining up the bottom edges of the pocket with the edge of the panel and pinning.

13. Assemble the patchwork as in **F**.

14. With a ¼in (6mm) seam allowance, machine sew the 5½ x 1in (14 x 2.5cm) strip to the left side of the left top pocket. Press all seams towards the narrow strips. Sew to the other top pocket. Sew the 10½ x 1in (26.7 x 2.5cm) strip to the top of the largest pocket. Sew the two panel halves together. Add side borders first, then top and bottom borders.

FINISHING THE HANGING

15. Place the front panel and backing fabric right sides together and pin all round. Machine sew with a ½in (1.3cm) seam allowance, leaving a 4in (10.2cm) gap at the centre of the lower edge. Trim off the corners within the seam allowance, but do not cut right up to the stitches – to about ⅛in (3mm). Turn the hanging right way out through the gap, easing out corners. Lay the panel flat and smooth. Turn under the raw edges at the bottom, pin or tack and slipstitch the gap closed. From the back, hand sew right round the panel ⅛in (3mm) from the edge with small stitches through backing and seam allowances only to keep the backing in place.

MAKING A HANGING SLEEVE:

16. Follow the section within Getting Started for making a hanging sleeve.

Long samplers

Small samples are a good way to practise new sashiko patterns and need not be forgotten in your work basket afterwards. Ready-made picture frames make a feature of your stitching for a lovely gift. Simple unvarnished frames and three different shades of indigo fabric were used for these samples. The narrow frames, just 10 x 4in (25.4 x 10.2cm), used up fabric oddments. Instructions are included for stitching larger areas of these patterns, which can also be resized by changing the original grid proportions. The size of your frame will dictate the size of your sashiko panel.

Sashiko patterns used asanoha, fundō and jūji kikkō

Finished size of samplers shown 10 x 4in (25.4 x 10.2cm)

You will need

» Small frame of your choice

» Piece of self-adhesive mounting card, same size as frame backing board

» Piece of sashiko fabric at least ½in (1.3cm) larger than frame size all round

» Several strands of medium sashiko thread per frame

» Basic sewing and marking kit

Commercial frame sizes normally refer to the size of the backing board or image rather than the measurement outside the moulding, eg a 6 x 4in (15.2 x 10.2cm) frame will fit a picture that size. Remember, the visible image area will be up to ¼in (6mm) smaller all round.

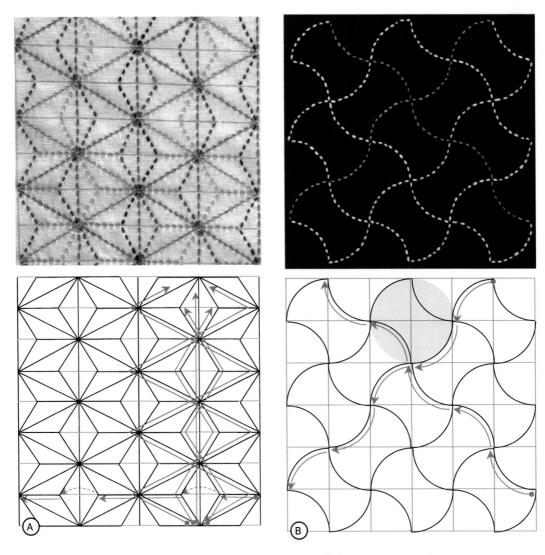

ASANOHA (HEMP LEAF)

This pattern is easier if you stitch the vertical lines and the large zigzag lines before you mark the shallow vertical zigzags. Take care not to let your stitches cross on the front where the pattern lines intersect.

Mark a grid – the stitched sample above is 1½in (3.2cm). Divide squares horizontally into rectangles. Mark the large zigzag lines only. Following the red arrows on **A** stitch the vertical lines (in red on the sample). Then stitch the diagonal lines as zigzags, forming figures of eight (light brown and yellow). Mark and stitch shallow vertical zigzags, also as figures of eight (dark brown and dark green). Finally, stitch the short horizontal lines (turquoise), keeping thread continuous and stranding across the back (red dashed lines).

FUNDŌ (SCALE WEIGHTS)

Mark a grid – the stitched sample above is 1in (2.5cm). The framed sample used a ½in (1.3cm) grid and a 1in (2.5cm) circle. To match the stitched sample shown here, use a 2in (5.1cm) circle template (shown in blue on **B**) to mark wavy lines. Following the red arrows, stitch diagonal wavy lines (red and light brown).

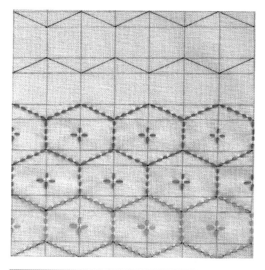

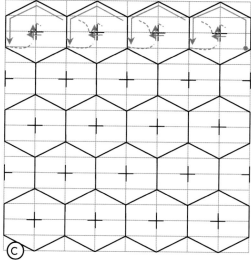

MARKING AND STITCHING THE SASHIKO

1. After carefully removing any glass in your picture frame, use the inside of the frame aperture to mark the working area on your fabric. Note how the patterns are resized to fit the frames. The asanoha pattern is stretched to fit, dividing the frame area into rectangles rather than squares to start. Select a design, mark it on the fabric (see Getting Started) and then stitch your sashiko using the instructions in this project and the advice in Getting Started.

FRAMING THE SAMPLERS

2. Lightly press your finished sashiko from the back. Arrange the sashiko on the self-adhesive mounting card, make sure the fabric grain is straight and then press the sampler into place.

3. Replace the glass in the picture frame and put the sashiko panel behind it. Replace any necessary packing in the back of the frame and fasten the grips in place.

JŪJI KIKKŌ (CROSS TORTOISESHELL)

This sashiko pattern is worked in rows. You may draw extra horizontal lines (optional) to keep the centre crosses straight.

Mark a grid – the stitched sample above is ⅜ x ¾in (1 x 1.9cm). The framed sample used a ¾ x ½in grid. Mark diagonal lines to form the tops of the hexagons. Following the red arrows on diagram **C**, stitch the pattern in rows, stitching around three sides of the hexagon (shown in red on the stitched sample), keeping the thread continuous and stranding across the back to stitch the centre crosses, indicated in the diagram by red dashed lines.

Ranru wall hanging

Stitch and create this stunning wall hanging, combining squares and rectangles of classic sashiko patterns. The subtle colours of a bundle of Indian shot cotton quilting scraps create a muted, vintage patchwork look.

Sashiko patterns used: asanoha (hemp leaf) variation, raimon (spiral) and masuzashi (square measure sashiko)

Finished size: 38 x 24in (96.5 x 61cm)

You will need

» Indian shot cotton, tsumugi or similar in various colours:
  › two pieces 10½ x 8½in (26.7 x 21.6cm) (1)
  › two squares 8½in (21.6cm) (2)
  › three pieces 8½ x 6½in (21.6 x 16.5cm) (3)
  › two squares 6½in (16.5cm) (4)
  › two pieces 8½ x 4½in (21.6 x 11.4cm) (5)
  › one piece 6½ x 4½in (16.5 x 11.4cm) (6)
  › one square 4½in (11.4cm) (7)
  › Two striped cotton squares 6½in (16.5cm) (8)

» Very narrow striped cotton for border:
  › two strips 24½ x 2½in (62.2 x 6.4cm),
  › two strips 34½ x 2½in (87.6 x 6.4cm)

» Plain cotton: 38½ x 24½in (96.5 x 62.2cm) for backing,
  › 24 x 8in (61 x 20.3cm) for hanging sleeve

» Muslin 38½ x 24½in (96.5 x 62.2cm) for wadding (batting)

» Fine or medium cream sashiko thread, large (100m) skein

» Sewing thread

» Basic sewing and marking kit

MAKING THE PATCHWORK

1. Lay out the patchwork pieces, using **A** as a guide.

2. The patches are labelled with letters in the You Will Need list. Machine sew patches together in pairs and strips, as indicated on the diagram using ¼in (6mm) seams throughout, pinning each seam as you go. For the final patchwork assembly, you will need to only partly sew some seams. Begin by sewing the striped square (8) to the bottom of the centre patchwork strip (2, 2), but sewing only 3in (7.6cm). Press the seam towards the centre strip. Add the strip of squares on the left (4, 3, 3) to the centre patchwork strip and sew the whole seam. From now on, press all new seams towards the piece you just added. Add the patchwork piece at the top of the panel. Add the right strip (6, 7, 3, 4). Add the bottom strip (7, 5). Add the bottom right patch (1). Now go back to the first seam that was only partly sewn and finish sewing it, overlapping the end of your previous stitches by about ½in (1.3cm). Press this seam towards the middle of the panel. Add the side borders next, then the top and bottom borders. Press towards the outside of the panel.

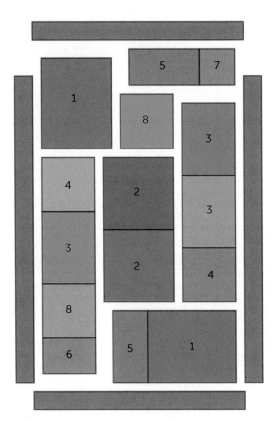

(A) Layout of all the patchwork pieces.

42

MARKING THE SASHIKO

3. Using the photograph as a guide mark the raimon **(B)**, masuzashi **(C)**, and asanoha **(D)** patterns in the relevant squares.

4. The space between lines for raimon and masuzashi is ½in (1.3cm). Use a quilters' ruler with parallel lines to mark the patterns. Start by drawing lines parallel to the sides of the patch and work inwards. Draw asanoha using **D**: quarter the rectangle equally into four smaller rectangles, then equally again into eight rectangles. Mark zigzag lines, as shown by the heavy black lines in diagrams c and d. Tack the patchwork panel to the muslin (see Getting Started).

STITCHING THE SASHIKO

Raimon: stitch the pattern in a spiral following the direction of the red arrow **(B)**.

Masuzashi: stitch the pattern from the outer square inwards, following the red arrow **(C)**. Cross the corners by one stitch and strand across the back to turn the corner, as indicated in the diagram by a red dashed line.

Asanoha: Stitch the sashiko, following the red arrows in c, d, and e on diagram **D**. Refer to the stitching tips within the Getting Started section. Press the completed panel.

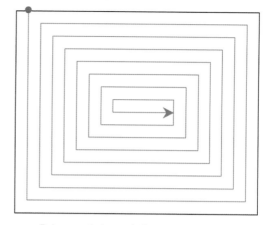

(B) Raimon spiral: mark the pattern beginning at the dot and following the direction of the red arrow.

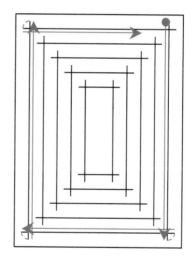

(C) Masuzashi: mark the pattern following the red arrows.

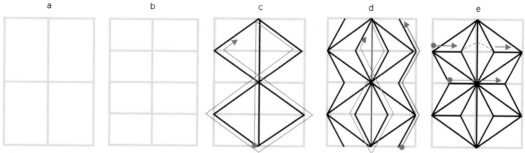

(D) Asanoha variation: The sequence for marking and stitching the pattern to fit a rectangle.

43

RANRU WALL HANGING

The Ranru Wall Hanging here has standard and distorted versions of asanoha (hemp leaf), raimon (spiral) and masuzashi (square measure sashiko). These patterns were changed by using the proportions of the outer shape, here a patchwork piece, as a starting point.

Raimon as a square and then as a rectangle

Masuzashi as a square

Asanoha repeated twice

Masuzashi as a rectangle

Stripes used to line up plain sashiko

Asanoha as a rectangle

Asanoha as a square

MAKING UP THE WALL HANGING

5. Place the front panel and backing fabric right sides together and pin all round. Machine sew with a ¼in (6mm) seam allowance, leaving an 8in (20.3cm) gap at the centre of the lower edge. Trim off the corners within the seam allowance, to about ⅛in (3mm) of the stitches. Turn through to the right side and ease the corners out so they are sharp. Lay the panel out flat and smooth. Turn under the raw edges at the bottom, pin or tack (baste) and slipstitch the gap closed. From the back, hand sew right round the panel ⅛in (3mm) from the edge with small stitches through backing and seam allowances only to keep the backing in place.

MAKING A HANGING SLEEVE

6. Follow the section in Getting Started for making a hanging sleeve.

About the Author

Susan Briscoe is a leading expert in the traditional Japanese sewing technique, sashiko. She was first introduced to sashiko in the early 1990s while teaching English in northern Japan where she learned the technique and studied the history of patchwork and quilting. Susan has published numerous books about sashiko and is regularly featured in patchwork and quilting magazines.

Suppliers

sewandsew
www.sewandso.co.uk
For threads, needles and notions

Stitchcraftcreate
www.stitchcraftcreate.co.uk
For fabrics and haberdashery

Euro Japan Links Ltd
www.eurojapanlinks.com

Japan Crafts
www.japancrafts.co.uk

E-quilter.com
www.equilter.com

BeBe Bold
www.bebebold.com

Index

A DAVID & CHARLES BOOK
© F&W Media International, Ltd 2016

David & Charles is an imprint of F&W Media International, Ltd
Pynes Hill Court, Pynes Hill, Exeter, EX2 5AZ

F&W Media International, Ltd is a subsidiary of F+W Media, Inc
10151 Carver Road, Suite #200, Blue Ash, OH 45242, USA

Text and Designs © Susan Briscoe 2016
Layout and Photography © F&W Media International, Ltd 2016

First published in the UK and USA in 2016

This edition is Printed on Demand for David & Charles, an F+W Media Inc. company

Susan Briscoe has asserted her right to be identified as author of this work in
accordance with the Copyright, Designs and Patents Act, 1988.

All rights reserved. No part of this publication may be reproduced in any form or by
any means, electronic or mechanical, by photocopying, recording or otherwise,
without prior permission in writing from the publisher.

A catalogue record for this book is available from the British Library.

ISBN-13: 978-1-4463-0632-1 paperback
ISBN-10: 1-4463-0632-1 paperback

ISBN-13: 978-1-4463-7461-0 PDF
ISBN-10: 1-4463-7461-0 PDF

ISBN-13: 978-1-4463-7462-7 EPUB
ISBN-10: 1-4463-7462-9 EPUB

10 9 8 7 6 5 4 3 2 1

Acquisitions Editor: Sarah Callard
Desk Editor: Michelle Patten
Project Editor: Jane Trollope
Art Editor: Anna Wade
Photographer: Jason Jenkins
Production Controller: Beverley Richardson

F+W Media publishes high quality books on a wide range of subjects.
For more great book ideas visit: www.stitchcraftcreate.co.uk

Layout of the digital edition of this book may vary
depending on reader hardware and display settings.

Made in the USA
Coppell, TX
21 September 2020

38567320R00031